A LITTLE
STYLE
BOOK

FRENCH STYLE

SUZANNE SLESIN
AND STAFFORD CLIFF

PHOTOGRAPHS BY
JACQUES DIRAND

CLARKSON POTTER/PUBLISHERS NEW YORK

Thank you again to all the people who allowed us to photograph their homes for French Style; *to our agent, Barbara Hogenson of the Lucy Kroll Agency; Kristin Frederickson and Beth Gardiner, our editorial assistants; Ian Hammond, our art associate; Howard Klein, art director of Clarkson Potter, and Renato Stanisic, designer; Joan Denman and Andrea C. Peabbles; and our editor, Roy Finamore, who made sure that this new* French Style, *although smaller in size, was just as consistently strong as the original.*

Published by Clarkson N. Potter, Inc./Publishers, 201 East 50th Street, New York, New York 10022.
Member of the Crown Publishing Group.
Random House, Inc. New York, Toronto, London, Sydney, Auckland.
CLARKSON N. POTTER, POTTER, and colophon are trademarks of Clarkson N. Potter, Inc.
Originally published by Clarkson N. Potter, Inc. in 1982.

Manufactured in China

Design by Renato Stanisic

Library of Congress Catalog Card Number 94-4808

ISBN 0-517-88214-0
10 9 8 7 6 5 4 3 2 1
Revised Edition

CONTENTS

INTRODUCTION

A sense of style is a primary French characteristic. It also, perhaps, underlies every foreigner's perception of the French. For decades, outsiders have had a distinct impression of French style as it is illustrated in French interiors.

Because an invitation to a French home is proverbially hard to come by, this image is a mirror of literary and historic accounts, visions that are both myth and reality: sympathetically cluttered or starkly empty rooms, which seem always to be warmly lighted and full of ambiance, with a carefully haphazard placement of furniture, well-patinated walls, silver glistening on the sideboard, and lace hung neatly at the windows.

Specific images spring to mind: the strikingly composed interiors of Degas's portraits; Vuillard's and Bonnard's richly evocative domestic scenes; the vibrant south of France window views by Matisse and Picasso—in which the view through the window itself and the way the scene is framed by the room are essential to the composition.

In the France re-created by artists, the exterior and the interior of the house are intimately joined, held in a special relationship. And these artists' images remain as representations of the France we remember. Past and present are interchangeable. The poetic countryside, the simple Parisian street scene, the rhythmic tree-lined boulevard, the lovely half-open window, are all frozen in time, yet we still very much want to believe in their existence.

Alongside this gentle and romantic perception of France, there has always been the fascination with an earlier and grander style, one inexorably linked to the image of France. This is the style of its kings and emperors, from Louis XIV to the Second Empire.

Today, in the same way that France's contemporary mores are a combination of past traditions and updated views, some of the best and most livable of French interiors represent a synthesis. The notion of regionalism has once again come into fashion, along with an appreciation of traditional everyday objects—the handsome rustic pottery, the chiaroscuro designs of the Jacquard Français linens, the flower-patterned hand-printed Provençal fabrics, the classic copper cookware.

For some, it is a celebration of local crafts and traditions. For others, it is a kind of adventurous tourism at home. Decorating never seems to start from scratch. Flea markets are scoured relentlessly and imaginatively. "You don't care what it is, you just buy what you like—it's emotional," says one Parisian. But one essentially Gallic talent quickly comes into play: a sense of how to arrange the objects to their best advantage. The French seem to delight in the design surprise—shapes are contrasted, periods clash, colors are in striking and atypical combinations. And it all looks effortless, as if it had just been done and yet had always been there.

Nor is a room ever considered finished. It's all a matter of rearranging as one goes along. In the home, the French joie de vivre *is a well-tempered* art de vivre.

PRECEDING PAGES: *A wrought-iron gate makes a rhythmic border for a spectacular view of Paris' Place des Vosges.*

LOOKING OUTSIDE

FOR both the French and the Francophiles, Paris has always been the center, the heart, the soul of the nation and its culture. Since the 19th century, it has been the very image of glamorous urban life. The grands boulevards of Paris and grandiose apartment buildings were conceived by city planner Baron Haussmann. They epitomize bourgeois urban life in the same way that the apartments themselves, with their spacious rooms, winding corridors, and molding-encrusted ceilings, embody the solidity and security of French family life.

Because neighborhoods developed at different times, it is not unusual to see façades of various architectural periods standing side by side—from the flowing sculptural details of the Art Nouveau period to the flat geometric fronts preferred by the modernists since the 1920s and 1930s.

In Paris and in the large cities of the provinces, only a few examples of the grand hôtels particuliers built by the rich nobility in the 18th century and the large private houses of the wealthy bourgeoisie in the late 19th and early 20th centuries have survived intact.

Like their counterparts in the United States, the urban French dream of finding the perfect country house. Situated in a village forgotten by time, down an untrodden path, or completely hidden in a forest, the house and its potager *embody the ideal of a simpler way of life—subsisting off the soil, retreating from urban crowds and pressures to the slower pace and firmer values of the past. These houses run the gamut from rustic to sophisticated, simple to grandiose.*

The romantic view of the bucolic life underscores the importance of the French countryside as it was celebrated by such 19th-century painters as Monet, Corot, and Pissarro, and by such early-20th-century photographers as Eugène Atget. "He wanted to record everything, everywhere, that spoke for a certain notion of France as an ancient civilization in which landscape, architecture and people lived together in total harmony," John Russell, the art critic, wrote of Atget in the New York Times.

PRECEDING PAGE: *The façade of the 18th-century manor house in Touraine has been covered with a beige-colored mixture of earth and sand from the Loire.*

EXTERIORS

PRECEDING PAGES: *The terraced houses in the medieval Provençal town of Gordes have thick walls that are a protection against heat and wind.* **ABOVE AND OPPOSITE:** *In the city or country, edged in stone,*

carved in wood, or engraved with decorative numbers, France's doors and doorways have always been one of the country's most stylish architectural elements.

18

ABOVE: *The grounds around the 16th-century Château de Thoiry have been transformed into a zoological garden.* **LEFT:** *The 1900 gray stone house in Monfort-l'Amaury was carefully renovated by fashion designer Chantal Thomass and her husband, Bruce.*

ABOVE: *Lace curtains are framed behind a green-shuttered cottage window.*
LEFT: *The symmetrical placement of the large-paned windows makes the façade of the Château de Thoiry look transparent.*

ABOVE AND OPPOSITE: *Whether it's an antique painted sign in Paris or a modern steel mile marker near the Massif Central, French signs command as much attention as the places to which they point.*

ABOVE AND OPPOSITE: *From the simplicity of a contemporary enamel panel to the elegance of antique ironwork or evocative mosaics, the designs of street and house numbers mark places with style.*

ABOVE: *A 19th-century house in a group of private villas in Paris has an exterior of white stone and red brick.*
RIGHT: *The view of the rooftops of Paris is one of the classic images of the city.*

28

The lace patterns on curtains that are often glimpsed behind glass windowpanes can be intricate or simple. The boldly worked cluster of crocheted grapes is an unusual variation.

*The façade of an 18th-
century stone house in
Bordeaux has been
cleaned and stands out
from its still-dark neighbors.
The tall windows, the ironwork, and the stonework
above the windows are
typical of the period.*

*The rugged stone façade
of a turn-of-the-century house
in the suburbs of Paris is
punctuated with delicate Art
Nouveau metalwork.*

RIGHT: *A street in suburban Paris displays the typical French mix of stone and brick buildings and lush greenery.*
BELOW: *A classically detailed doorway has become overgrown with vines.*

34

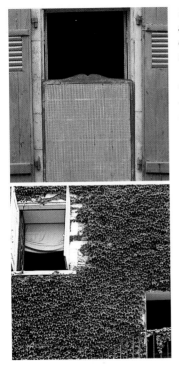

Windows from the Parisian suburbs to the Pyrénées display a variety of architectural and ornamental styles. Whether in the small windows of stone country houses or the more generously proportioned windows of urban residences, there is always something of interest to catch the eye.

LEFT: *The early-20th-century building in Paris is one of a series of unusual ateliers built for artists at the turn of the century. The tiled and ornamented façade is striking.*
BELOW: *The curved mosaic-tiled entrance to an apartment building conveys the Moorish-style decoration favored at the beginning of the 20th century.*

The exterior of this mid-18th-
century castle, near Les Baux
in Provence, has been kept
intact. The red tile is typical
of the region.

An 18th-century house in the Corrèze, with its earth-grouted walls and shuttered windows, has retained its original simplicity.

ABOVE: *A bird perches on the tiled roof of a country house where the window appears to be carved out of the roof.* **RIGHT:** *The curved red tiles on the roof of a Provençal house reflect the hot summer sun and protect the house from strong winds.*

RIGHT: *The eccentric neo-classic colonnaded entrance to the late-18th-century château in the south of France was inspired by the work of Italian Baroque architects.* **BELOW:** *The rusticated stone doorway contrasts with the delicate carving of an antique door.*

In French doorways, wood is a particularly well-worked material, whether because of the shape of the windowpanes it delineates or in the graceful detailing that is added to a country-house entrance.

Metalwork often reflects the period in which it was wrought, from the geometric Art Deco style to the more lyrical Art Nouveau decoration.

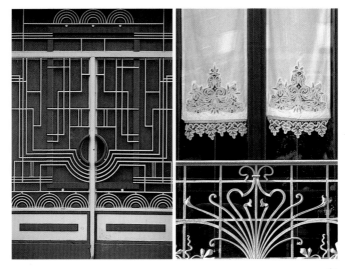

GARDENS

ABOVE: *The grounds around the 16th-century Château de Thoiry have been designed so as to focus on a dramatic fountain and parterres of grass.* **PRECEDING PAGES:** *The geometrically clipped topiary shrubs and low colorful flower beds are part of the formal approach to a small-scale traditional French garden.*

BELOW: *The landscaped roof garden of interior designer Andrée Putman's Paris loft has been shielded to provide a protected environment for plants that might often be seen in a more southern climate.*

ABOVE: *The gentle Touraine landscape is glimpsed through the arched windows of Pacha Bensimon's 18th-century manor house.*
RIGHT: *A birdcage and a collection of kitchen gadgets form a still life on a stone wall under one of the small windows of this converted barn in the Roussillon.*

The terrace situated at the back of artist César Baldacini's Mediterranean-style villa near St. Paul de Vence has a floor of inlaid marble. The chairs surrounding the table—some cast-iron, some rattan—are deliberately mismatched. A large umbrella of unbleached linen provides shade.

LEFT: *The lush garden behind a Paris home, with its charming assortment of white chairs, delivers a welcome respite from the bustle of the heavily trafficked city street only yards away.*
BELOW: *The double stone archway at the Château de Varengeville in Normandy beckons with an enticing glimpse of lush green.*

The relationship between house and garden can be punctuated
with such things as the glass-enclosed veranda at Jean Lafont's
home in the Camargue region, **ABOVE LEFT,** the table made from
an old church clockface, **ABOVE RIGHT,** in interior decorator Dick

Dumas's garden in the south of France, the flourishing Virginia creeper that covers the façade of Eric and Xiane Germain's Paris house, **ABOVE LEFT,** *and the antique wood column that is set in the doorway to an old garden in the south of France,* **ABOVE RIGHT.**

Looking Inside

UNLIKE the British, whose famous bow windows seem to invite glimpses into the home, the French tend to shield themselves from the outside world. Traditionally, sheer or lace curtains allowed light to come in during the day, yet afforded a certain amount of privacy; drawing the thick double drapes was an evening ritual. Most windows are not without decorative interest and act as introductions to well-ordered and charmingly appointed interiors.

From the era of Louis XV until the early 1960s, there were few significant changes in the French living room. Called the salon, it was the room where one received guests and where important family questions were presented for serious discussion. Television was one catalyst for changing the salon into a multipurpose room, as was the simultaneous discovery of the big, comfy sofa, which allowed for relaxation and informality. And when shrinking residential spaces made the two rooms one, it was not unusual to designate a coin repas as well as a coin salon.

The French kitchen was traditionally reigned over by the women of the household. While mores have changed, the kitchen remains a focus of the home, whether it is small and citified and equipped with the bare essentials or an expansive cluttered country kitchen with a checkered floor, cast-iron stove, and open shelves for china.

Bedrooms continue to be not only for sleeping but places in which to retreat, dine, and think. Literary references reinforce the image. Marcel Proust received visitors while in bed; Colette wrote surrounded by cats in her bed overlooking the gardens of Paris's Palais Royal.

In France collecting is not so much a hobby as a way of life. Drawing from flea markets and antiques shops, as well as their grandmothers' attics, collectors can transform the plainest pieces of pottery and glass, the most common knickknacks, into engaging works of art simply by the way they display them in their homes.

PRECEDING PAGES: *In a Paris apartment, a low gray marble table is flanked by a large terra-cotta urn from Vallauris. An Aubusson-style rug is in the foreground.*

LIVING

LEFT: *A large rustic wood table has been placed in front of the fireplace in Pacha Bensimon's Touraine manor house. The 18th-century wing chair has been stripped and reupholstered in a country-style printed fabric.* **PRECEDING PAGES:** *The pale yellow living room walls of Bernard and Laura Ruiz-Picasso's apartment act as a backdrop for a collection of works by Bernard's grandfather, Pablo Picasso. The leather chairs are by Le Corbusier; the mantelpiece has been painted to resemble lapis lazuli.*

ABOVE: *A bowl of carved wood fruit sits in a flared-arm chair from the 1930s in Agnès Comar's Paris living room.* **FAR LEFT:** *Rough textured walls are an appropriate backdrop for this mix of flowers.* **LEFT:** *The mantel of a black-and-white tiled fireplace is used to display a collection of flea-market finds.*

Above and overleaf: *The strong sun of the Bordeaux region is filtered through wood shutters in one of the city's most beautiful 18th-century town houses. The deep bergère armchairs were found in the family's attic. Some have been painted white and reupholstered, others simply slipcovered in white canvas.* **Left:** *The* grand salon *in Emmanuelle and Quasar Khanh's house has been furnished with leather-covered chairs by Auguste Perret, the architect who designed the 1930s house.*

A gilt-edged, cream satin upholstered armchair takes center stage in the classical 18th-century Paris living room of Paloma Picasso and Raphael López-Sanchez.

ABOVE LEFT: *The carved wood mantel is topped with an antique rustic scene.* **ABOVE RIGHT:** *The tall mirror and tiled fireplace are original to a 1900 house outside Paris.* **RIGHT:** *A Venetian mirror hangs over the fireplace, which is painted white to match the rest of the space.*

The curtains and loose slipcovers in artist and furniture designer
Mattia Bonetti's Paris living room were made from cotton sheeting.
The wrought-iron grille is from a shop window display.

ABOVE: *An antique bed is used as a freestanding sofa in the center of fashion designer Louise de la Falaise's Paris studio apartment.* **RIGHT:** *Fashion designer Karl Lagerfeld chose to deflate the formality of his library with stacks of books and magazines piled on the table and the floor.*

ABOVE: *A book by Cecil Beaton, an anonymous German photograph, and a neoclassic gray-and-red painted chair create an intriguing still life.* **LEFT:** *The wall paneling and window frames in Chantal and Bruce Thomass's Monfort l'Amaury house were stripped and lightened. The old-fashioned flowers emphasize the feeling of nostalgia in the room.*

82

LEFT: *A combination of mismatched bentwood and bamboo chairs furnish a room.* **ABOVE:** *The desk in Andrée Putman's Paris loft is an Art Deco black lacquer piece with ivory inlays. The carpet is by Eileen Gray.* **OVERLEAF:** *In Putman's loft, antique Thonet bentwood chairs surround a mirrored table from the 1930s.*

ABOVE: *Josef Hoffmann designed this bentwood settee, side chairs, and lounge chairs for J. J. Kohn in about 1905; they now furnish Eric Philippe and Léonore Bancilhon's Paris apartment.*
RIGHT: *In the same apartment, the blond linden wood suite, which dates from about 1910, might be by Otto Prutscher.*

LEFT: *Architect George Candilis's collection of bentwood furniture is exceptional because of the quality and number of pieces he has managed to assemble under one roof. The dining room, with its small settees, dining chairs, and tables, is completely, even traditionally, furnished with bentwood.* **OVERLEAF:** *Garden designer and writer Madison Cox's Paris living room has been furnished with overscale, plush, tapestry-covered seating.*

ABOVE: *A mix of bentwood and wicker furnishes César Baldacini's white-walled living room.* **RIGHT:** *The Art Deco chaise longue is upholstered in soft pink velvet, traditionally reserved for more classical pieces.*

Louise de la Falaise decoratively drapes pieces of brocaded and woven antique Chinese textiles over the mezzanine railing in her Paris apartment.

A soft blue velvet–upholstered sofa with a swan-shaped frame was chosen by a Paris illustrator for its graceful contours.

Huge earthenware containers full of dried lavender are placed on the tile floor in front of the arched windows of a renovated barn in the Rousillon. The table is covered with a cloth of local patchwork.

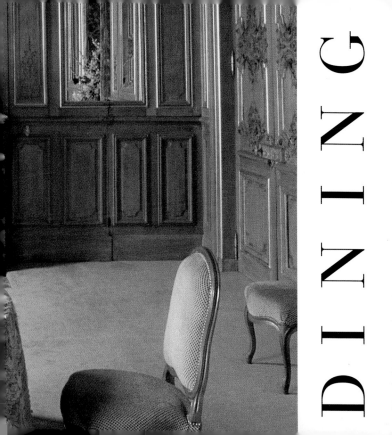

DINING

LEFT: *The dining room of Monique Petit's suburban Paris house is furnished with a round table covered with a fringed and tasseled quilted cloth. The original parquet floors are kept bare.* **PRECEDING PAGES:** *In fashion designer Karl Lagerfeld's exquisite 18th-century dining room, Louis XV furniture is placed as it would have been in the past. For extra historical ambiance, candles are lit on the mantel.*

In the Paris apartment of fashion designer Jean-Charles de Castelbajac and his wife, Catherine, a round table and round-backed chairs echo the shape of the unusual mouse gray room, which has a window set in a rounded wall. The other side of the room is squared off.

The paneled walls, antique lace tablecloth, wicker chairs, and fabric and bead lamp from the 1920s contribute to the nostalgia and charm of Nadine and Etienne Roda-Gil's Paris dining room. Early-20th-century floral motifs were the inspiration for the painted decorative friezes on the wall.

Jacqueline Dufour's Paris dining room is focused around a large turn-of-the-century Renée Marval painting of a reclining woman. A lamp from about 1900 is set on a late-19th-century antique brass table in front of a Jean Dunand screen painted with swallows. The wrought-iron table and chairs from the 1930s were found in an antiques shop.

Set off against a stripped pine floor in a Paris house are an oval dining table, bentwood chairs with seats incised in an iris pattern, and a bowl of carved fruit.

ABOVE: *Viscount and Viscountess de Thoiry's antique china is a cherished heirloom but is used often by the family to create a sense of history.* **LEFT:** *In Monique Petit's suburban Paris home, tea is often taken in a magical grotto, a kind of winter garden filled with plants and wicker furniture.*

The pink-hued ocher walls soften the large dining room of the Château de Thoiry. Many of the furnishings, including the elaborate serving dishes and the busts, have been in the castle for more than four hundred years.

On the Ile de Ré across from the town of La Rochelle, the fresh-looking kitchen with its antique marble tabletop is where most meals are taken. The cupboard once held paper and supplies in a notary's office.

Although each of the plates on the dining table in this 18th-century manor house in Touraine is different, and some are even chipped, they form a satisfying composition. The kitchen with its antique stove is open to the room.

ABOVE: *Healthy plants flourish in a light-filled Paris dining room that has been furnished with a long wood table and vintage bistro chairs.* **RIGHT:** *The traditional marble-topped buffet came originally from a bakery. It is now used as a sideboard to hold silverware and dishes as well as groups of shapely pears and apples set on cake stands.*

In this dining room, the parquet floors have been highly polished but kept bare. The table is covered with a piece of white oilcloth. The 1930s chairs originally belonged to the owner's parents.

*Antique outdoor metal chairs
and a table—all painted white
—are set up for eating in this
veranda room. The serving
buffet and the patterned floor
are both made of stone.*

121

The kitchen in this turn-of-the-century house has been furnished with antique cherry wood chairs and a marble-topped bistro table. The tile floor is new. The spice cupboard by the refrigerator was found in Amsterdam.

COOKING

126

ABOVE: *Dishes and groceries are stored in a large cupboard built into an alcove in whitewashed stone walls.* **LEFT:** *A tiny summer-house kitchen has a deep double sink. Spoons and implements are kept on the windowsill.* **PRECEDING PAGES:** *The wood-burning ovens in the ancient kitchen of the 16th-century Château de Chazeron, in Auvergne, are made from local volcanic stone.*

The kitchen in Daniel Rozensztroch's renovated Paris loft is small but well organized, with industrial wire shelving set directly into the wall.

ABOVE: *Antique ceramic containers and a coffeepot are some of the accessories in a Paris kitchen.* **RIGHT:** *In Kim and Odile Molzter's Paris kitchen, a Provençal cloth covers the table. The checkered floor is traditional. A shiny stainless steel restaurant stove has been installed near a still-working antique cast-iron unit.*

Copper pots, a whisk, a wire salad basket, an antique scale, and other tools hang from a ceiling rack in a château kitchen.

A knife rack is conveniently hung near the impressive black cast-iron stove in this Paris kitchen. Some of the bread is trompe l'oeil ceramic.

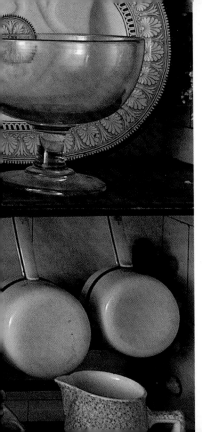

In Monique Petit's suburban Paris kitchen, pieces of antique china, well-worn enamel pots, and flea-market finds are displayed against a wall of pleasantly cracked white tiles.

ABOVE: *In the kitchen of a mid-18th-century château in Provence, glass jars are lined up over the roomy fireplace.*
RIGHT: *The huge black cast-iron stove, while functional, also offers a visual focus to a high-ceilinged Paris kitchen.*

Above: *In fashion designer Corinne Bricaire's Paris kitchen, stove and cooktop are incorporated into the custom-made cast-iron table, over which hangs a large custom hood.* **Right:** *The kitchen, with its traditional checkered floor, of this renovated stone house is seen through the pantry door.*

The walls and fireplace of the large country-house kitchen in the Roussillon are made of the red stone typical of the region. The table and chairs are simple country items, and baskets and bottles are mixed with peasant wares.

Under a small window, dishes drip dry in an old stone sink that has a drain leading directly to the outside, typical in many rustic houses.

SLEEPING

ABOVE: *In a tiny country bedroom, a small step stool serves as a bedside table and a piece of fabric hangs on the wall in lieu of a headboard.* **RIGHT:** *The wallpaper matches the handblocked Souleiado Provençal fabric used for the bedcover.* **PRECEDING PAGES:** *François Baudot, a decorator, designed a canopied tent structure for his Paris bedroom using white cotton sheets.*

Above: *Interior decorator Jacques Grange created a neo-Egyptian bedroom out of a theater set by customizing the theater flats to fit the walls of a Parisian bedroom and making a four-poster bed out of the columns.* **Right:** *A painted and lacquered bed from the 1880s, with a lace-edged pillow and embroidered bedcover, furnishes a child's bedroom.*

One of the guest rooms in Jean Lafont's house in the south of France features a 1930s decor and includes a bed by Pierre Chareau, as well as pieces by Jean-Michel Frank. A series of photographs, including a portrait of Marie-Laure de Noailles by Man Ray, are hung like paintings along two walls.

The intimate master bedroom in Jacques Grange's Paris apartment, done in muted shades, recalls the atmosphere of Postimpressionist Edouard Vuillard's paintings. The bedcover is made of antique cashmere; the carpet is Turkish; a screen acts as a headboard.

BELOW: *In Monique Petit's Paris bedroom, the bed, table, and chair are covered with quilted white fabric.* **RIGHT:** *An Italian rococo-style shell table sits next to the antique bed in Louise de la Falaise's Paris studio.*

LEFT: *One of the bedrooms in Pacha Bensimon's country manor house achieves near-monastic serenity. The walnut-frame bed is covered with an Irish coverlet; the walls are decorated with bunches of grasses and heather that recall the surrounding countryside.* **OVERLEAF:** *Ornate doors open onto Karl Lager-feld's Paris bedroom. The classically appointed interior includes a museum-quality Louis XVI bed, signed Jacob, with a canopy of rich French embroidered fabric. Stereo headphones are at hand on the modern lamp.*

160

ABOVE: *A bedroom that overlooks Paris's Jardin de l'Observatoire is furnished in a garden theme. There is a trellis on one wall, a green-and-white quilt on the bed, and a wicker chair in front of the open window.* **RIGHT:** *In a bedroom in the French countryside, the antique metal bed frame is painted pale yellow and the bedside table is covered with an embroidered white cotton tablecloth.*

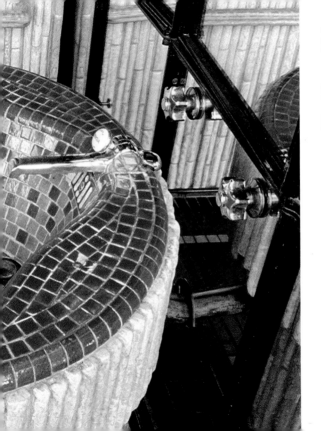

BATHING

166

Above: *The stuccoed walls have been worked in a swirling pattern in a country-house bathroom.* **Left and preceding pages:** *The bathroom in photographer Jean-Luc Buyo's Paris apartment was originally designed by cabinetmaker and interior designer Jules Leleu in 1932. The organically shaped sink is of red and gold mosaic tile, and the walls are of ceramic elements that imitate bamboo.*

167

ABOVE: *An antique cane folding chaise stands near an old claw-footed bathtub painted in trompe l'oeil marble.* **RIGHT:** *The bath in Jean Lafont's house has an enclosure covered in 18th-century multicolor tiles set on the diagonal.*

FAR LEFT: *Ivory-handled toilette articles are grouped on the small wicker table in a suburban bathroom.*
LEFT: *The oval marble bathtub in the Gothic-style master bathroom dates from the 19th century.*

ABOVE: *In César Baldacini's master bathroom, pieces of mirror added to white tile create a shimmery effect on the walls.* **LEFT:** *The bathtub and sink in a bathroom designed by Jacques Grange were originally in an old Parisian hotel.*

The tiles in Jacques
Grange's bathroom are
from the 19th century, and
the pink flamingo is a 1900
lithograph from a bistro.

In a bathroom in Touraine, the walls are tinted deep rose to contrast with the locally made white porcelain fixtures.

176

For this Paris house, Andrée Putman chose Italian white ceramic tiles for the floor, walls, and tub. The faucets and the hardware look old, but they are modern nickel-plated reproductions. The long radiator, a necessity in large bathrooms, was installed under the windows to visually echo the venetian blinds.

COLLECTING

THESE AND PRECEDING PAGES: *Once mass-produced, original bentwood is now rare and prized by collectors. Architect George Candilis stores his bentwood treasures in an 1840 building in the Montparnasse area of Paris. Rocking chairs, which first appeared in Europe right after the middle of the 19th century, as well as a bonanza of side chairs and lounge chairs, are displayed in rooms throughout the house.*

The cubistic painting and the row of small sculptures and mineral samples create a series of busy patterns that are offset against the paneling of this room.

An off-center composition on a marble mantelpiece is dominated by the wood-framed picture of a small boy.

The master bedroom in Jean Lafont's home is dedicated to his collection of romantic Gothic furniture. A series of chairs stands on a 19th-century petit-point rug that depicts an imaginary and extravagant Gothic cathedral.

ABOVE: *The squareness of a plain white mantel contrasts with the rhythmic succession of circular plates and the softness of the dried flowers.* **RIGHT:** *The simple effect of placing three white plates on a mantelpiece is based on a contrast of different textures—wood, brick, and china—all in the same brown-and-white palette.*

A group of shiny globes
and striking black-framed
photographs creates a
striking still life on a night
table in a Paris apartment.

A specialist's assemblage of antique seals and boxes is geometrically displayed on a side table.

Two antique sailing boats are displayed on a rectangular Le Corbusier table in the luminous white-walled foyer of painter Valerio Adami's Paris apartment.

A gardenlike display of flowers in small glass vases can create a color focus for a sideboard.

A natural-hued still life includes a painting on glass of a mustachioed gentleman from the turn of the century, a series of baskets and boxes, and small bisque figurines.

Above: *A collection of antique glass bottles surrounded by bunches of dried field flowers provides a lyrical French country still life.*
Left: *Clear glass bowls and decanters, wineglasses, and water glasses are conveniently stored on the white shelves of a vacation-house kitchen.*

ABOVE: *Monique Petit's collection of giant insects rests in a glass case.* **RIGHT:** *A wicker chair filled with seashells is one of artist César Baldacini's baroque and poetic accumulations of objects.*

ABOVE: *A cluster of old pitchers and bowls is left outside on a table.* **RIGHT:** *Plain all-white china is assembled in a dark wood cabinet.* **FAR RIGHT:** *A wood cabinet in a country house in the south of France is filled with area pottery and favorite objects made by area craftsmen.*

RIGHT: *Bowls and plates made by local craftsmen, and cutlery used for eating out of doors, are left to dry on a garden table in the Roussillon.* **BELOW:** *Wood hat forms and pottery pitchers are part of an eclectic grouping of earth-toned objects displayed against a brick wall.*

202

ABOVE LEFT: *Trompe l'oeil terra-cotta objects are arranged on a mantel under a Cubist painting.* **ABOVE RIGHT:** *Chantal Thomass keeps her collection of accessories in a glass-topped table in the dressing room.* **LEFT:** *A collection of antique canes is displayed just inside the front door of this Paris home.*

Cadum

PIERO MANZONI

LEFT AND FAR LEFT: *The shelves in the house of the artist known as Ben are used to display a very eccentric collection of objects that include advertising memorabilia and Art Deco figurines.* **OVERLEAF:** *A Japanese mask and a 19th-century Chinese mannequin, along with two large shells, form an arresting display in an illustrator's Paris apartment.*

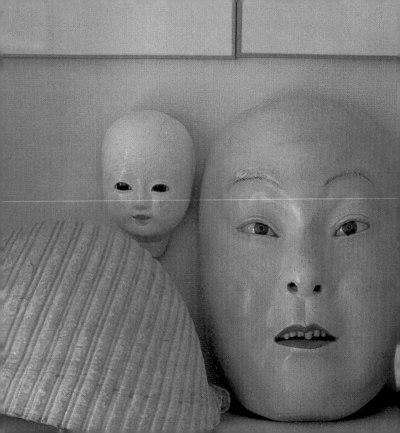

Other titles in the series